MO

D0727614

home

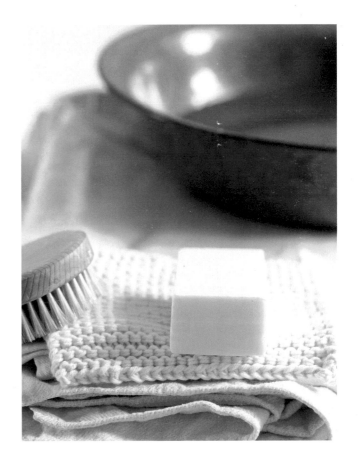

Middlesbrough Libraries

0061299219

home
debbie bliss

27 knitted designs for living

MIDDLESBROUGH LIBRARIES & INFORMATION

0061299219

EBURY PRESS
LONDON

DEDICATION

To the memory of Tommie

AB		MM	
MA		MN	
MB		MO	1\06
MC		MR	
MD		MT	
ME		MW	
MG			
MH			

First published in Great Britain in 2005

1 3 5 7 9 10 8 6 4 2

Text © Debbie Bliss 2005
Photographs © Pia Tryde 2005

Debbie Bliss has asserted her right to be identified as the author of this work under the Copyright, Designs and Patents Act 1988.

All rights reserved. No part of this publication may be reproduced, stored in a retrieval system, or transmitted in any form or by any means, mechanical, photocopying, recording or otherwise, without the prior permission of the copyright owners.

First published by Ebury Press
Random House, 20 Vauxhall Bridge Road, London SW1V 2SA

Random House Australia (Pty) Limited
20 Alfred Street, Milsons Point, Sydney, New South Wales 2061, Australia

Random House New Zealand Limited
18 Poland Road, Glenfield, Auckland 10, New Zealand

Random House South Africa (Pty) Limited
Endulini, 5A Jubilee Road, Parktown 2193, South Africa

The Random House Group Limited Reg. No. 954009

www.randomhouse.co.uk

A CIP catalogue record for this book is available from the British Library.

Editor: Emma Callery
Designer: Christine Wood
Photographer: Pia Tryde
Stylist: Julia Bird
Pattern checker: Rosy Tucker
Charts: Anthony Duke

ISBN 0 091 903599

Papers used by Ebury Press are natural, recyclable products made from wood grown in sustainable forests.

Printed and bound in Singapore by Tien Wah Press

contents

Introduction 6 ♥ Knitting essentials 8

introduction

Home is a celebration of the art of homemaking. Whether you spend time in a stylish loft apartment, a country cottage or a seaside beach hut, making decorative or practical handknits creates an individual and personal touch that makes your house a home.

To reflect our different lifestyles, the projects are divided into three sections: *Urban*, *Modern Country* and *Seaside*.

The projects in *Urban* are worked in strong, graphic colours and with geometric shapes and spot patterns that sing out against the pared-down shapes and style of the contemporary house. A spotted bedspread or cushions in clashing shades will add a vibrant note to any room and a lime felted bag and colourful gloves are the perfect accessories to enliven a drab day in town.

Modern Country reflects the rural landscape with contemporary knits worked in natural yarns in russets, taupes and browns, including a soft moss stitch wrap to snuggle into and a cosy jacket. For new or basic knitters, there are easy starter projects, such as a garter stitch washcloth and moss stitch pan holder.

In *Seaside*, the knits take on a nautical theme with floor cushions and throws for picnics on the beach or deck, worked in crisp cottons and using stitch patterns that evoke the classic fisherman's Guernseys. A ribbed, casual jacket and a simple sweater for a child are ideal for a relaxed holiday wardrobe.

The *Home* collection includes knits that cover a range of knitting skills, from very easy to projects for the more advanced knitter. Happy homemaking.

knitting essentials

following pattern instructions

Figures for larger sizes are given in round ( ) brackets. Where only one figure appears, this applies to all sizes. Work the figures given in square [ ] brackets the number of times stated afterwards. Where 0 appears, no stitches or rows are worked for this size. As you follow the pattern, make sure that you are consistently using the right stitches for your size – it is only too easy to switch sizes inside the brackets. One way to avoid this is to photocopy the instructions first and mark off the figures for the size you are knitting with a coloured marker or highlighter.

The quantities of yarn quoted in the instructions are based on the yarn used by the knitter for the original garment and amounts should therefore be considered approximate. A slight variation in tension can make the difference between using less or more yarn than that stated in the pattern. Before buying the yarn, look at the measurements in the knitting patterns to be sure which size you want to knit. My patterns quote the actual finished size of the garment, not the chest size of the wearer. The length of the garment is taken from the shoulder shaping to the cast-on edge.

tension

Each pattern in the book states a tension or gauge – the number of stitches and rows per centimetre or inch that should be obtained with the given needles, yarn and stitch pattern. Check your tension carefully before starting work. A slight variation in tension can spoil the look of a garment and alter the proportions that the designer wanted. A too loose tension will produce uneven knitting and an unstable fabric that can droop or lose its shape after washing, while too tight a tension can create a hard, unforgiving fabric.

To make a tension square, use the same needles, yarn and stitch pattern quoted in the tension note in the pattern. Knit a sample at least 12.5cm/5in square. Smooth out the finished sample on a flat surface but do not stretch it. To check the stitch tension, place a tape measure horizontally on the sample and mark 10cm/4in with pins. Count the number of stitches between pins. To check the row tension, place the tape measure vertically on the sample and mark 10cm/4in. Count the number of rows between the pins. If the number of stitches and rows is greater than that stated in the pattern, try again using larger needles. If the number of stitches and rows is less, use smaller needles. If you are only able to obtain either the stitch or the row tension, it is the stitch tension that is the most important to get right, as the length of many patterns are calculated by measurement rather than the number of rows you need to work to achieve it.

garment care

Taking care of your handknits is important. If you have invested all that time and labour into knitting them, you want them to look good for as long as possible.

Check the yarn label for washing instructions. Most yarns can now be machine washed on a delicate wool cycle. Prior to washing, make a note of the measurements of the garment or accessory, such as the width and length. After washing, lay the knitting flat and check the measurements again to see if they are the same. If not, smooth and pat it back into shape.

Some knitters prefer to hand wash their knits. Use soap flakes specially created for hand knits, and warm rather than hot water. Handle the knits gently in the water – do not rub or wring, as this can felt the fabric. Rinse well to get rid of any soap, and squeeze out excess water. You may need to get rid of more water by rolling the knitting in a towel, or use the delicate spin cycle of the washing machine. To dry the knitting, lay it out flat on a towel to absorb moisture, and smooth and pat it into shape. Do not dry knits near direct heat, such as a radiator. Store your knits loosely folded to allow the air to circulate.

needle conversion chart

This needle conversion chart covers all the knitting needle sizes used for the patterns in this book.

UK metric	US sizes	UK metric	US sizes
2¾mm	size 2	4½mm	size 7
3mm	size 2–3	5mm	size 8
3¼mm	size 3	5½mm	size 9
3¾mm	size 5	6½–7mm	size 10½
4mm	size 6	7½–8mm	size 11

standard abbreviations

alt = alternate

beg = beginning

cm = centimetres

cont = continue

dec = decreas(e)ing

foll = following

in = inches

inc = increas(e)ing

k = knit

kfb = k into front and back of st

kfpb = knit into front and purl into back of next st to make one st

m1 = make one by picking up loop lying between st just worked and next st and working into the back of it

p = purl

patt = pattern

pfb = purl into front and back of next st

pfkb = purl into front and knit into back of next st to make one st

rem = remain(ing)

rep = repeat

skpo = slip 1, knit 1, pass slipped stitch over

sl = slip

st st = stocking stitch

st(s) = stitch(es)

tbl = through back of loop

tog = together

yf = yarn to front of work

types of yarns

wool   Wool spun from the fleece of sheep is the yarn that is the most commonly associated with knitting. It has many excellent qualities, as it is durable, elastic and warm in the winter. Wool yarn is particularly good for working colour patterns, as the fibres adhere together and help prevent the gaps that can appear in Fair Isle or intarsia.

Some knitters find that a simple stitch such as moss stitch or garter stitch can look neater when worked in a wool rather than a cotton yarn.

cotton   Cotton yarn, made from a natural plant fibre, is an ideal all-seasons yarn, as it is warm in the winter and cool in the summer. I particularly love to work in cotton because it gives a clarity of stitch that shows up subtle stitch patterning, such as a moss stitch border on a collar or cuffs.

cotton and wool   Knitting in yarn that is a blend of wool and cotton is particularly good for children's wear. This is because the wool fibres give elasticity for comfort but, at the same time, the cotton content is perfect for children who find wool irritating against the skin.

cashmere   Cashmere is made from the underhair of a particular Asian goat. It is associated with the ultimate in luxury, and is unbelievably soft to the touch. If combined with merino wool and microfibre, as in my cashmerino yarn range, it is perfect for babies and children as well as adults.

buying yarn   Always try to buy the yarn quoted in the knitting pattern. The designer will have created the design specifically with that yarn in mind, and a substitute may produce a garment that is different from the original. For instance, the design may rely for its appeal on a subtle stitch pattern that is lost when using a yarn of an inferior quality, or a synthetic when used to replace a natural yarn such as cotton will create a limp fabric and the crispness of the original design will be lost. We cannot accept responsibility for the finished product if any yarn other than the one specified is used.

substituting yarns   If you do decide to use a substitute yarn, buy one that is the same weight and, where possible, has the same fibre content. It is essential to use a yarn that has the same tension as the original or the measurements will change. You should also check metreage or yardage – yarn that weighs the same may have different

lengths so you may need to buy more or less yarn. Check the ball band on the yarn. Most yarn labels now carry all the information you need about fibre content, washing instructions, weight and metreage or yardage.

It is essential to check the dye lot number on the yarn label. Yarns are dyed in batches or lots, which can sometimes vary quite considerably. Your retailer may not have the same dye lot later on, so try and buy all your yarn for a project at the same time. If you know that sometimes you use more yarn than that quoted in the pattern, buy more. If it is not possible to buy the amount you need all in the same dye lot, work the borders or the lower edges in the odd one since the colour change is less likely to show here.

Debbie Bliss yarns

The following are descriptions of my yarns and a guide to their weights and types. Most of the yarns used in the designs are machine washable, but always check the ball band for details. (See page 126 for yarn distributors.)

Debbie Bliss merino double knitting: a 100% merino wool in a double-knitting weight. Soft to the touch but hardwearing. Approximately 110m/50g ball.

Debbie Bliss merino aran: a 100% merino wool in an Aran or fisherman weight. Approximately 78m/50g ball.

Debbie Bliss cashmerino aran: a 55% merino wool, 33% microfibre, 12% cashmere yarn in an Aran or fisherman weight. A luxurious yarn with a beautiful handle. Approximately 90m/50g ball.

Debbie Bliss baby cashmerino: a 55% merino wool, 33% microfibre, 12% cashmere lightweight yarn between a 4-ply and a double knitting. Approximately 84m/50g ball.

Debbie Bliss cashmerino superchunky: a 55% merino, 33% microfibre, 12% cashmere yarn in a superchunky weight. Knits up quickly on larger needles. Approximately 75m/50g ball.

Debbie Bliss cotton double knitting: a 100% pure cotton that knits up to slightly thicker than a standard double knitting tension. Approximately 84m/50g ball.

Debbie Bliss cotton denim aran: knits to an Aran or fisherman weight. A soft and light, non-shrinking denim-look yarn. Approximately 68m/50g ball.

Debbie Bliss alpaca silk: an 80% alpaca, 20% silk yarn that knits to an Aran weight. Approximately 65m/50g ball.

Debbie Bliss maya or SoHo: a 100% handspun wool slub that knits up between an Aran and chunky weight. Approximately 126m/100g hank for Maya and 65m/50g ball for SoHo.

urban

humbug cushion

This is an unusual three-dimensional triangular cushion, which is firmly stuffed to

make it a great backrest. For a larger version, just add stitches and rows.

size

Approximate height 42cm/16½in.

materials

Six 50g balls of Debbie Bliss cotton dk in

Chocolate

Pair 4mm (US 6) knitting needles

45 x 84cm/17¾ x 33in of cotton lining fabric

Polystyrene beads

tension

19 sts and 28 rows to 10cm/4in square over

patt using 4mm (US 6) needles.

abbreviations

cm = centimetres

cont = continue

in = inches

k = knit

p = purl

patt = pattern

st(s) = stitch(es)

to make With 4mm (US 6) needles, cast on 82 sts.

1st row (right side) K5, [p2, k5] to end.

2nd row Purl.

These 2 rows form the patt and are repeated throughout.

Cont in patt until work measures 82cm/32¼in, ending with a p row.

Cast off.

to make With right sides together and taking 1cm/½in seams throughout, stitch together
lining the short sides of fabric piece to form a tube. Fold the tube flat with the seam to
one side and join from the seam to the fold at one end. Open out the unstitched
end and refold the fabric so the first seam lies centrally, and stitch the seam,
leaving 5cm/2in unstitched at one end. Turn through to the right side and fill with
polystyrene beads. Stitch the opening closed.

to make Join cast-on and cast-off edges of knitted piece to form a tube. Fold the tube
up flat with the seam to one side and join from the seam to the fold at one end.
Open out the unstitched end and insert the filled lining, then stitch the seam
closed so that the first seam lies centrally.

medium spot cushion

A large spot on a basic cushion makes a dramatically bold statement against a neutral background.

size
Approximately 45cm/16in square.

materials
Four 50g balls of Debbie Bliss merino dk in Chocolate and one 50g ball in Lime
Pair 4mm (US 6) knitting needles
45cm/16in square cushion pad

tension
22 sts and 30 rows to 10cm/4in square over st st using 4mm (US 6) needles.

abbreviations
cm = centimetres
in = inches
k = knit
st st = stocking stitch
st(s) = stitch(es)

note
When working motif, use separate balls of yarn for each area of colour and twist yarns together on wrong side to avoid holes.

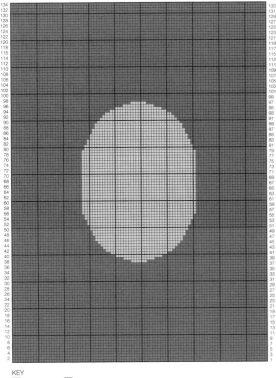

front With 4mm (US 6) needles and Chocolate, cast on 98 sts.
Beg with a k row, work 134 rows in st st from Chart.
Cast off.

back With 4mm (US 6) needles and Chocolate, cast on 98 sts.
Beg with a k row, work 134 rows in st st.
Cast off.

to make up Join three sides of Back and Front together, insert cushion pad and join remaining seam.

KEY
 Chocolate Lime

gloves

Fingertips of colour give a touch of fun to a classic pair of gloves. The cashmere mix yarn makes them soft as well as warm.

measurements
To fit medium hands.

materials
One 50g ball of Debbie Bliss baby cashmerino in Teal (A) and Pale Lilac (B) and small amounts of Dark Lilac (C), Pink (D), Red (E) and Green (F)
Pair each 3mm (US 2–3) and 3¼mm (US 3) knitting needles

tension
25 sts and 34 rows to 10cm/4in square over st st using 3¼mm (US 3) needles.

abbreviations
alt = alternate
beg = beginning
cm = centimetres
cont = continue
foll = following
in = inches
inc = increas(e)ing
k = knit
m1 = make one by picking up loop lying between st just worked and next st and working into the back of it
p = purl
rem = remain(ing)
rep = repeat
st st = stocking stitch
st(s) = stitch(es)
tog = together

right glove   ** With 3mm (US 2–3) needles and A, cast on 44 sts.

Rib row [K1, p1] to end.

Rep the last row 23 times more and inc 6 sts evenly across last row. 50 sts.

Change to 3¼mm (US 3) needles and B.

Beg with a k row, work in st st.

Work 4 rows **.

Thumb shaping

Next row K25, m1, k3, m1, k22.

Work 3 rows.

Next row K25, m1, k5, m1, k22.

P 1 row.

Next row K25, m1, k7, m1, k22.

P 1 row.

Next row K25, m1, k9, m1, k22.

P 1 row.

Cont to inc as set on next and 2 foll alt rows. 64 sts.

P 1 row.

Divide for thumb

Next row K42, turn.

Next row P17, turn and cont on these sts only.

Work 14 rows in st st.

Change to C.

Work 4 rows.

Next row K1, [k2tog] to end.

Break yarn, thread through rem 9 sts, draw up tightly and join seam.

With right side facing, rejoin B to base of thumb, k to end. 47 sts.

Work 13 rows.

*** **Divide for fingers**

First finger

Next row K30, turn and cast on 2 sts.

Next row P15, turn.

Work 18 rows in st st.

Change to D.

Work 4 rows.

Next row K1, [k2tog] to end.

Break yarn, thread through rem 8 sts, draw up tightly and join seam.

Second finger

With right side facing, rejoin B to base of first finger, pick up and k2 sts from base of first finger, k6, turn, cast on 2 sts.

Next row P16, turn.

Work 22 rows in st st.

Change to A.

Work 4 rows.

Next row [K2tog] to end.

Break yarn, thread through rem 8 sts, draw up tightly and join seam.

Third finger

With right side facing, join B to base of second finger, pick up and k2 sts from base of second finger, k6, turn, cast on 2 sts.

Next row P16, turn.

Work 18 rows in st st.

Change to E.

Work 4 rows.

Next row [K2tog] to end.

Break yarn, thread through rem 8 sts, draw up tightly and join seam.

Fourth finger

With right side facing, join B to base of third finger, pick up and k2 sts from base of third finger, k5, turn.

Next row P12.

Work 12 rows in st st.

Change to F.

Work 4 rows.

Next row [K2tog] to end.

Break yarn, thread through rem 6 sts, draw up tightly and join seam down to cast-on edge.

left glove   Work as given for Right Glove from ** to **.

Thumb shaping

Next row K22, m1, k3, m1, k25.

Work 3 rows.

Next row K22, m1, k5, m1, k25.

P 1 row.

Next row K22, m1, k7, m1, k25.

P 1 row.

Next row K22, m1, k9, m1, k25.

P 1 row.

Cont to inc as set on next and 2 foll alt rows. 64 sts.

P 1 row.

Divide for thumb

Next row K39, turn.

Next row P17, turn and cont on these sts only.

Work 14 rows in st st.

Change to C.

Work 4 rows.

Next row K1, [k2tog] to end.

Break yarn, thread through rem 9 sts, draw up tightly and join seam.

With right side facing, rejoin B to base of thumb, k to end. 47 sts.

Work 13 rows.

Complete as for Right Glove from *** to end.

big spot and diamond cushions

For a strong look, these cushions combine geometric patterning in stripes,

diamonds and a spot. For a calmer look, you could try using neutral shades.

big spot cushion

size
Approximately 45cm/16in square.

materials
Three 50g balls of Debbie Bliss merino dk in
Red and two 50g balls in Pink
Pair 4mm (US 6) knitting needles
45cm/16in square cushion pad

tension
22 sts and 30 rows to 10cm/4in square over
st st using 4mm (US 6) needles.

abbreviations
beg = beginning
cm = centimetres
in = inches
k = knit
st st = stocking stitch
st(s) = stitch(es)

note
When working motif, use separate balls of
yarn for each area of colour and twist yarns
together on wrong side to avoid holes.

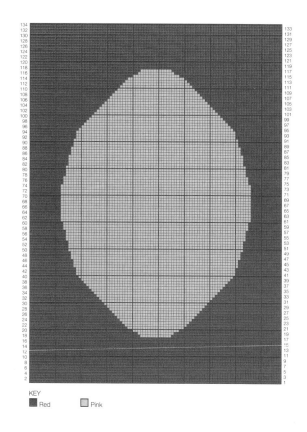

KEY
■ Red   ☐ Pink

front   With 4mm (US 6) needles and Red, cast on 98 sts.
Beg with a k row, work 134 rows in st st from Chart.
Cast off.

back   With 4mm (US 6) needles and Pink, cast on 98 sts.
Beg with a k row, work 134 rows in st st, working in 2 row stripes of Pink and Red.
Cast off in Pink.

to make up   Join three sides of Back and Front together, insert cushion pad and join remaining seam.

diamond cushion

size
Approximately 45cm/16in square.

materials
Two 50g balls of Debbie Bliss merino dk in
each of Red and Pink
Pair 4mm (US 6) knitting needles
45cm/16in square cushion pad

tension
22 sts and 30 rows to 10cm/4in square over
st st using 4mm (US 6) needles.

abbreviations
cm = centimetres

cont = continue

in = inches

k = knit

p = purl

patt = pattern

rep = repeat

st st = stocking stitch

st(s) = stitch(es)

chart notes
Read right side (k) rows from right to left and
wrong side (p) rows from left to right. When
working motifs, use separate balls of yarn for
each area of colour and twist yarns together
on wrong side to avoid holes.

front　With 4mm (US 6) needles and Pink, cast on 98 sts.
Beg with a k row, work in st st from Chart as follows:
1st to 4th rows Work in st st.
5th row K first 9 sts of Chart, work the 16 st patt repeat 5 times, then k the last
9 sts of Chart.
6th row P first 9 sts of Chart, work the 16 st patt repeat 5 times, then p the last
9 sts of Chart.
The 5th and 6th rows set the Chart.
Cont to work all 26 Chart rows.
Rep 1st to 26th rows four times more, then 1st to 4th rows again.
Cast off.

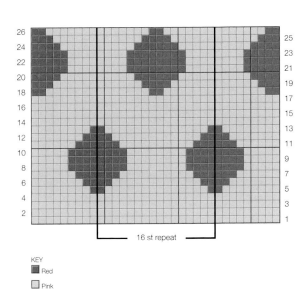

16 st repeat

KEY
■ Red
□ Pink

back   With 4mm (US 6) needles and Red, cast on 98 sts.
Beg with a k row, work in st st until 134 rows have been worked.
Cast off with Red.

to make   Join three sides of Back and Front together, insert cushion pad and join
up   remaining seam.

plaited scarf

This unusual scarf is easier to make than it looks. After knitting, the simple ribbed

pieces are plaited and secured to make a colourful accessory.

size
Approximately 125cm/49in long.

materials
One 100g ball of Debbie Bliss cashmerino
superchunky in each of Pale Lilac, Lime
and Plum
Pair 7½mm (US 11) knitting needles

tension
18 sts and 16 rows to 10cm/4in square over
unstretched rib, using 7½mm (US 11) needles.

abbreviations
cm = centimetres
in = inches
k = knit
p = purl
st(s) = stitch(es)

strip   (Make 3, one in each shade)

With 7½mm (US 11) needles, cast on 11 sts.

1st row (right side) K1, [p1, k1] to end.

2nd row P1, [k1, p1] to end.

These 2 rows form the rib and are repeated.

Work in rib until strip measures approximately 137cm/54in.

Cast off in rib.

to make   Lay the three strips side by side on a flat surface and stitch the edge of the first
up   5cm/2in of each strip to the next. Keeping the strips flat, plait them together and stitch the edge of the last 5cm/2in of each strip to the next. Using the odd ends of yarn, catch stitch together the strips where they cross.

socks with cables

Handknitted socks in a cashmere mix will add a touch of luxury when you want to take time out and cosy up on a sofa or armchair in front of the television or with a good book.

size
One size to fit shoe size UK 4–6/US 5–7.

materials
Two 50g balls of Debbie Bliss baby cashmerino in Lilac
Set of 4 double-pointed 3¼mm (US 3) knitting needles

tension
25 sts and 34 rows to 10cm/4in square over patt using 3¼mm (US 3) needles.

abbreviations
alt = alternate
beg = beginning
C4F = slip next 2 sts onto a cable needle and hold at front of work, k2, then k2 from cable needle
C4B = slip next 2 sts onto a cable needle and hold at back of work, k2, then k2 from cable needle
cm = centimetres
cont = continue
dec = decreas(e)ing
foll = following
in = inches
k = knit
p = purl
patt = pattern
rem = remain(ing)
rep = repeat
skpo = slip 1, knit 1, pass slipped stitch over
sl = slip
st st = stocking stitch
st(s) = stitch(es)
tog = together

to make

(make 2)

With 3¼mm (US 3) double-pointed needles, cast on 54 sts.

Distribute sts evenly, with 18 sts on each of 3 needles.

Work in rounds as follows:

Rib round *K1, p1; rep from * to end.

Rep the last round 5 times more.

Work in patt as follows:

1st round K11, p1, k4, p1, k21, p1, k4, p1, k10.

2nd round As 1st round.

3rd round K11, p1, C4B, p1, k21, p1, C4F, p1, k10.

4th to 6th rounds As 1st round.

These 6 rounds form the patt and are repeated.

Cont in patt until sock measures 20cm/8in, dec one st over each cable and working 2 sts tog at end of last round. 51 sts.

Cut yarn.

Shape heel

Slip next 13 sts onto first needle, next 13 sts onto second needle, next 13 sts onto 3rd needle and last 12 sts onto end of first needle.

Rejoin yarn to beg of first needle.

Next row K24, turn.

Next row Sl 1, p22, turn.

Next row Sl 1, k21, turn.

Next row Sl 1, p20, turn.

Cont in this way, working one st less on every row until the foll row has been worked:

Next row Sl 1, p10, turn.

Then work as follows:

Next row Sl 1, k11, turn.

Next row Sl 1, p12, turn.

Cont in this way, working one st more on every row until the foll row has been worked:

Next row Sl 1, p24, turn.

** Slip next 17 sts onto first needle, next 17 sts onto second needle and next 17 sts onto 3rd needle.

Cont in rounds of st st until sock measures 14cm/5½in from **, dec one st at end of last round. 50 sts.

Shape toe

Next round [K1, skpo, k19, k2tog, k1] twice.

Next round K to end.

Next round [K1, skpo, k17, k2tog, k1] twice.

Next round K to end.

Next round [K1, skpo, k15, k2tog, k1] twice.

Next round K to end.

Cont in rounds, dec on every alt round as set until the foll round has been worked:

Next round [K1, skpo, k7, k2tog, k1] twice. 22 sts.

Slip first 11 sts onto one needle and rem 11 sts onto a second needle.

Fold sock inside out and cast off one st from each needle together.

spot blanket

Vibrant spots in clashing colours create an area of vibrancy against the cool

minimalism of this contemporary bedroom.

size
Approximately 116 x 183cm/45½ x 72in.

materials
Nineteen 50g balls of Debbie Bliss merino
aran in Red and eighteen balls in Pink
Pair 5mm (US 8) knitting needles
4.00mm crochet hook

tension
18 sts and 24 rows to 10cm/4in square over
st st using 5mm (US 8) needles.

abbreviations
ch = chain

cm = centimetres

dc = double crochet in UK

in = inches

k = knit

p = purl

rep = repeat

st st = stocking stitch

st(s) = stitch(es)

chart notes
Read right side (k) rows from right to left and
wrong side (p) rows from left to right. When
working motif, use separate balls of yarn for
each area of colour and twist yarns together
on wrong side to avoid holes.

first panel
With 5mm (US 8) needles and Red, cast on 32 sts.
Beg with a k row, work in st st from Chart.
Work 1st to 40th rows from Chart, working circle motif in Pink.
Change to Pink.
Beg with a k row, work in st st from Chart.
Work 1st to 40th rows from Chart, working circle motif in Red.
Rep the last 80 rows four times more and 1st to 40th rows again.
Cast off in Red.

second panel
With 5mm (US 8) needles and Pink, cast on 32 sts.
Beg with a k row, work in st st from Chart.
Work 1st to 40th rows from Chart, working circle motif in Red.
Change to Red.
Work 1st to 40th rows from Chart, working circle motif in Pink.
Rep the last 80 rows four times more and 1st to 40th rows again.
Cast off in Pink.

third, fifth and seventh panels
Work as First Panel.

fourth and sixth panels
Work as Second Panel.

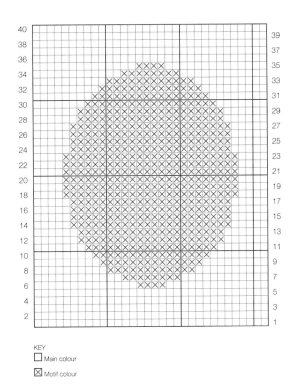

KEY
☐ Main colour
☒ Motif colour

to make up   Join the panels together so that the edge of the Second Panel is joined to the edge of the First, the edge of the Third is joined to the Second, and so on. Edging: With right side facing and 4.00mm crochet hook, join Red to any corner and work as follows: 2ch (stands as 1st dc), work dc all round outer edge of blanket, join with a slipstitch. Fasten off.

felted bag

This bag is knitted in an alpaca silk yarn, so that even after felting it retains a

beautiful softness.

size
Approximately 31 x 31cm/12¼ x 12¼in.

materials
Seven 50g balls of Debbie Bliss alpaca silk in
Lime
5mm (US 8) circular needle

tension
18 sts and 24 rows to 10cm/4in square over
st st before felting, using 5mm (US 8) needles.

abbreviations
beg = beginning
cm = centimetres
cont = continue
in = inches
inc = increas(e)ing
k = knit
kfb = k into front and back of st
p = purl
st st = stocking stitch
st(s) = stitch(es)

note
You may find it easier to work the base using
a pair of 5mm (US 8) needles and then
change to the circular needle to work the main
bag.

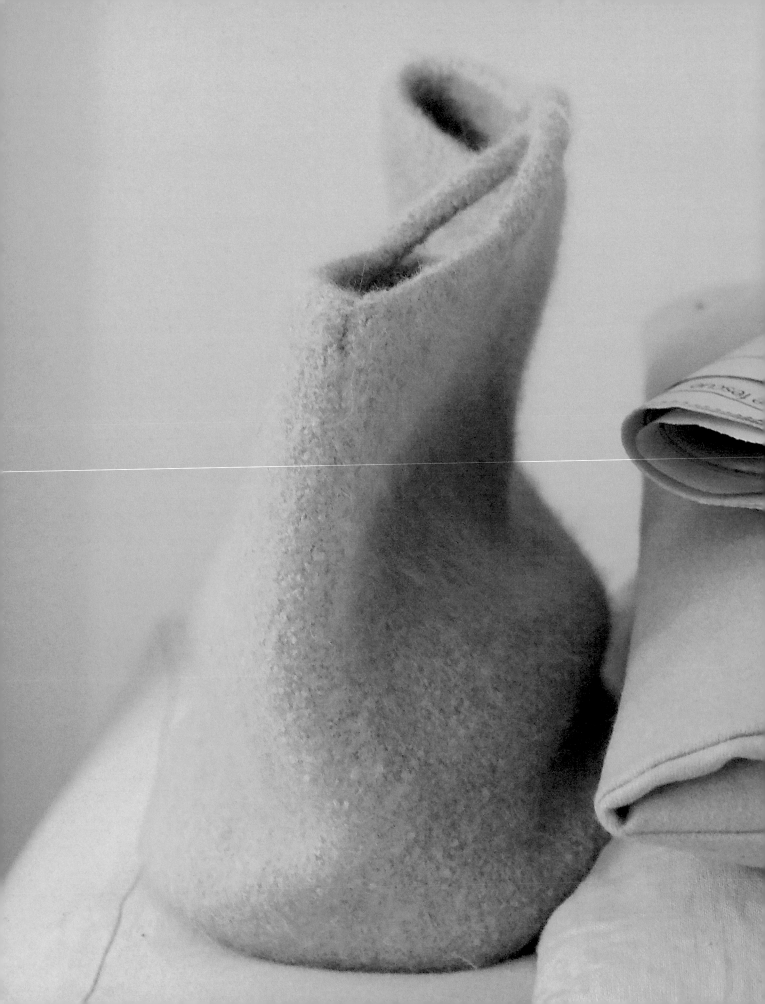

base   With 5mm (US 8) circular needle, cast on 5 sts.

1st row (right side) [Kfb] 4 times, k1. 9 sts.

2nd and all wrong side rows Purl.

3rd row [Kfb] 8 times, k1. 17 sts.

5th row [K1, kfb] 8 times, k1. 25 sts.

7th row [K2, kfb] 8 times, k1. 33 sts.

9th row [K3, kfb] 8 times, k1. 41 sts.

Cont to work in st st and inc 8 sts across every right side row as set, working one st more before each inc as before until there are 137 sts, ending with a right side row.

main bag   **1st ridge row** (wrong side) Knit.

2nd ridge row (right side) Purl.

Beg with a p row, work in st st until bag measures 43cm/17in from 2nd ridge row, ending with a k row.

Next row (wrong side) Knit.

Next row Purl.

Next row K21, cast off 26, k next 41 sts, cast off 26, k to end.

Next row (right side) Purl and cast on 26 sts over each set of 26 sts cast off in previous row.

Next row Knit.

Next row Purl.

Next row Cast off knitwise.

to make   Join seam from top edge to ridge row, then across the base.
up   Darn in all yarn ends.

to felt the   Place the knitted bag into the washing machine with other
bag   objects (I used old training shoes tied inside a pillowslip) and wash on the highest heat setting with the maximum spin speed. When removed from the machine, gently pull into shape and leave to dry.

modern country

cable and moss stitch bag

A chunky cable decorates this multi-coloured bag, which is lined with gingham fabric to give it extra durability. It makes a great little bag for carrying your knitting around.

size
Approximately 22cm/8¾in wide x 15cm/6in high excluding handles.

materials
Two 100g hanks of Debbie Bliss maya or four 50g balls of Debbie Bliss SoHo in shade 09
Pair each 8mm (US 11) and 5½mm (US 9) knitting needles
0.5m/½yd lining fabric
Sewing thread
60cm/24in polythene tubing

tension
12 sts and 16 rows to 10cm/4in square over st st using 8mm (US 11) needles and yarn used double.

abbreviations
C8B = slip next 4 sts onto cable needle and hold at back of work, k4, then k4 from cable needle

C8F = slip next 4 sts onto cable needle and hold at front of work, k4, then k4 from cable needle

cm = centimetres

in = inches

k = knit

kfb = knit into front and back of next st to make one st

kfpb = knit into front and purl into back of next st to make one st

p = purl

pfkb = purl into front and knit into back of next st to make one st

rep = repeat

st(s) = stitch(es)

tog = together

to make With 8mm (US 11) needles and double yarn, cast on 29 sts.

1st row K1, [p1, k1] to end.

2nd row As 1st row.

3rd row (right side) K1, p1, k1, k7, [kfb] 4 times, p1, [kfb] 4 times, k7, k1, p1, k1. 37 sts.

4th row K1, p1, k1, p15, k1, p15, k1, p1, k1.

5th row Pfkb, p1, k1, k7, C8B, p1, C8F, k7, k1, pfkb, p1. 39 sts.

6th row [P1, k1] twice, p15, k1, p15, [k1, p1] twice.

7th row [P1, k1] twice, k15, p1, k15, [k1, p1] twice.

8th to 12th rows Rep 6th and 7th rows twice more and 6th row again.

13th row Kfpb, k1, p1, k1, k7, C8B, p1, C8F, k7, k1, p1, kfpb, k1. 41 sts.

14th row K1, [p1, k1] twice, p15, k1, p15, k1, [p1, k1] twice.

15th row K1, [p1, k1] twice, k15, p1, k15, k1, [p1, k1] twice.

16th to 20th rows Rep 14th and 15th rows twice more and 14th row again.

21st row Pfkb, [p1, k1] twice, k7, C8B, p1, C8F, k7, k1, p1, k1, pfkb, p1. 43 sts.

22nd row [P1, k1] 3 times, p15, k1, p15, [k1, p1] 3 times.

23rd row [P1, k1] 3 times, k15, p1, k15, [k1, p1] 3 times.

24th to 28th rows Rep 22nd and 23rd rows twice more and 22nd row again.

29th row Kfpb, k1, [p1, k1] twice, k7, C8B, p1, C8F, k7, [k1, p1] twice, kfpb, k1. 45 sts.

30th row K1, [p1, k1] 3 times, p15, k1, p15, k1, [p1, k1] 3 times.

Shape for base

31st row (right side) Cast off 7 sts, k next 14 sts, p1, k15, k1, [p1, k1] 3 times.

32nd row Cast off 7 sts, p next 14 sts, k1, p15. 31 sts.

33rd row K15, p1, k15.

34th row P15, k1, p15.

Rep the last 2 rows 4 times more.

43rd row (right side) Cast on 7 sts and work k1, [p1, k1] 3 times across these sts, k15, p1, k15.

44th row Cast on 7 sts, work k1, [p1, k1] 3 times across these sts, p15, k1, p15, k1, [p1, k1] 3 times. 45 sts.

45th row (right side) K1, [p1, k1] 3 times, k15, p1, k15, k1, [p1, k1] 3 times.

46th row K1, [p1, k1] 3 times, p15, k1, p15, k1, [p1, k1] 3 times.

47th row P2tog, k1, [p1, k1] twice, k7, C8B, p1, C8F, k7, [k1, p1] twice, k1, p2tog. 43 sts.

48th row [P1, k1] 3 times, p15, k1, p15, [k1, p1] 3 times.

49th row [P1, k1] 3 times, k15, p1, k15, [k1, p1] 3 times.

50th to 54th rows Rep 48th and 49th rows twice more and 48th row again.

55th row K2tog, [p1, k1] twice, k7, C8B, p1, C8F, k7, [k1, p1] twice, k2tog. 41 sts.

56th row K1, [p1, k1] twice, p15, k1, p15, k1, [p1, k1] twice.

57th row K1, [p1, k1] twice, k15, p1, k15, k1, [p1, k1] twice.

58th to 62nd rows Rep 56th and 57th rows twice more and 56th row again.

63rd row P2tog, k1, p1, k1, k7, C8B, p1, C8F, k7, k1, p1, k1, p2tog. 39 sts.

64th row [P1, k1] twice, p15, k1, p15, [k1, p1] twice.

65th row [P1, k1] twice, k15, p1, k15, [k1, p1] twice.

66th to 70th rows Rep 64th and 65th rows twice more and 64th row again.

71st row K2tog, p1, k1, k7, C8B, p1, C8F, k7, k1, p1, k2tog. 37 sts.

72nd row K1, p1, k1, p15, k1, p15, k1, p1, k1.

73rd row K1, p1, k1, k7, [k2tog] 4 times, p1, [k2tog] 4 times, k7, k1, p1, k1. 29 sts.

74th row K1, [p1, k1] to end.

75th row As 74th row.

Cast off in moss st.

handles

(make 2)

With 5½mm (US 9) needles and a single length of yarn, cast on 7 sts.

Moss st row K1, [p1, k1] 3 times.

Rep the last row until strip measures 34cm/13½in.

Cast off in moss st.

to make up

Lay the bag flat onto the lining fabric and use as a template to cut the lining, allowing an extra 1.5cm/⅝in of fabric all around. Make up the knitted bag by joining the side seams from the cast-on/cast-off edges down to the base shaping. Sew cast-off/cast-on edges of base shaping to row ends of base. Make up lining in the same way. Sew 3cm/1¼in of each end of the handle strips to the inside of the front and the back of the bag. Cut the polythene tubing into two 30cm/12in lengths and make a 2cm/¾in diagonal cut across each end of the two pieces. Make 2 holes in each end of the tubing pieces and use these to stitch the tubing to the inside of the bag where the handles have been attached. Fold the handles around the tubing and stitch the seam. Insert the lining into the bag and slipstitch around the top edge, so hiding the ends of the handles.

cabled slippers

Knitted slippers are great for relaxing in around the house. Knitted in cotton with cables, they are a sturdier alternative to socks.

sizes

To fit sizes   UK 4–5/US 5–6   UK 6–7/US 7–8

materials

2(3) 50g balls of Debbie Bliss cotton dk in Terracotta
Pair 4mm (US 6) knitting needles
Pair of insoles the appropriate size
Lining fabric and fabric glue

tension

20 sts and 28 rows to 10cm/4in square over st st using 4mm (US 6) needles.

abbreviations

C4B = slip next 2 sts onto a cable needle and hold at back of work, k2, then k2 from cable needle

C4F = slip next 2 sts onto a cable needle and hold at front of work, k2, then k2 from cable needle

Tw2L = k into back of 2nd st on left needle, k into front of 1st st, then slip both sts off left needle together

Tw2R = k into front of 2nd st on left needle, k into front of 1st st, then slip both sts off needle together

beg = beginning

cm = centimetres

cont = continue

dec = decreas(e)ing

foll = following

in = inches

inc = increas(e)ing

k = knit

p = purl

patt = pattern

rem = remain(ing)

st(s) = stitch(es)

tog = together

note

The slippers are worked in one piece, starting with the upper and working towards the toe, then working the sole, ending at the heel. Sizings are approximate, as knitted fabric is elastic.

left slipper

Upper

With 4mm (US 6) needles, cast on 68(74) sts.

1st row (right side) P8(11), [Tw2R, p3] 3 times, [k4, p5] twice, k4, [p3, Tw2R] 3 times, p8(11).

2nd row K8(11), [p2, k3] 3 times, [p4, k5] twice, p4, [k3, p2] 3 times, k8(11).

3rd row Cast off 3 sts, p next 4(7) sts, [Tw2R, p3] 3 times, [C4B, p5] twice, C4B, [p3, Tw2R] 3 times, p8(11).

4th row Cast off 3 sts, k next 4(7) sts, [p2, k3] 3 times, [p4, k5] twice, p4, [k3, p2] 3 times, k5(8). 62(68) sts.

These 4 rows set the position of the twist sts and cables.

Cont in patt and cast off 4 sts at beg of next 4 rows and then 3 sts at beg of foll 0(2) rows. 46 sts.

Next row P2tog, patt to last 2 sts, p2tog. 44 sts.

Patt 5(3) rows.

Next row K2tog, k1, p3, Tw2R, p3, C4B, p3, p2tog, C4B, p2tog, p3, C4B, p3, Tw2R, p3, k1, k2tog. 40 sts.

Next row [P2, k3] twice, p4, [k4, p4] twice, [k3, p2] twice.

Patt 4 rows as now set, working cables on 3rd of these 4 rows.

Next row K2tog, p3, Tw2R, p3, k4, p2, p2tog, k4, p2tog, p2, k4, p3, Tw2R, p3, k2tog. 36 sts.

Cont in patt and dec one st at each end of 4th(6th) and foll 4th(6th) row and then of every foll 4th row until 24 sts rem.

Patt 1(3) rows.

Cast off 2 sts at beg of next 6 rows and 3 sts at beg of foll row. 9 sts.

Next row (wrong side) Cast off 3 sts, p1, p2tog, p1, k1. 5 sts.

Sole

Moss st row K1, [p1, k1] twice.

(Rep this row once more for Right Slipper only.)

Next row Inc in first st, moss st to last st, inc in last st. 7 sts.

Moss st 1 row.

Rep the last 2 rows 5(6) times more. 17(19) sts.

Work 20(22) rows in moss st.

Next row Work 2tog, moss st to end.

Moss st 3 rows.

Rep the last 4 rows 2(3) times more. 14(15) sts.

Moss st 28(30) rows.

Cast off 2 sts at beg of next 4(6) rows. 6(3) sts.

Cast off.

right slipper

Work exactly as for Left Slipper, working C4F for C4B and Tw2L for Tw2R and noting bracketed addition.

to make up

Making sure that slippers are mirror images, join ends of cast-on edge and row ends of 1st row together to form centre back seam. Slipstitch sole to upper around edge. Using the insoles as templates, cut out two pieces of fabric allowing an extra 1cm/½in all around the edge. Cover the insoles with fabric, turn the excess onto the underside and glue in place. Slip the insoles into the slippers, and catch in place with a few stitches.

felted cosies

Create a contemporary classic with a modern take on the tea cosy. Felted after

knitting, this teapot warmer is both practical and stylish.

sizes

Tea cosy to fit a medium sized teapot.

Egg cosy (not shown) to fit a medium sized

egg in an eggcup

materials

Tea cosy – Four 50g balls of Debbie Bliss

alpaca silk in Coral

Egg cosy – One 50g ball per 2 cosies

Pair 5mm (US 8) knitting needles

Contrast yarn for pompon

tension

18 sts and 24 rows to 10cm/4in square over

st st, before felting, using 5mm (US 8)

needles.

abbreviations

alt = alternate

cm = centimetres

dec = decreas(e)ing

foll = following

in = inches

k = knit

rem = remain(ing)

st st = stocking stitch

st(s) = stitch(es)

tbl = through back of loop

tog = together

note

Before washing/felting, the cosy will appear to

be far too big, but the fabric will shrink.

to make **tea cosy** (make 2 halves)	With 5mm (US 8) needles, cast on 67 sts. K 1 row. Beg with a k row, work 30 rows in st st. **Shape top** **Next row** (right side) K2tog tbl, k to last 2 sts, k2tog. Cont in st st and dec one st as set at each end of 7 foll 4th rows, then 2 foll alt rows. P 1 row. Cast off 2 sts at beg of next 8 rows, then 4 sts at beg of foll 6 rows. Cast off rem 7 sts.

to make **egg cosy** (not shown) (make 2 halves)	With 5mm (US 8) needles, cast on 22 sts. K 1 row. Beg with a k row, work 12 rows in st st. **Shape top** **Next row** (right side) K2tog tbl, k to last 2 sts, k2tog. Cont in st st and dec one st as set at each end of 4 foll 4th rows. 12 sts. P 1 row. Cast off 2 sts at beg of next 4 rows. Cast off rem 4 sts.

to felt the **fabric**	Darn in all yarn ends. Place knitted pieces into the washing machine with other objects (I used old training shoes tied inside a pillowslip) and wash on the highest heat setting with the maximum spin speed. When removed from the machine, gently unroll the felted fabric pieces around the edges, pull into shape and leave to dry flat.

to make **up**	Place the two felted pieces together and stitch around the shaped edge, leaving the cast-on edges open. Make a pompon from contrast yarn (see opposite) and sew to top of cosy.

pompon

1   Cut two circles from cardboard that are slightly smaller than the diameter of the pompon required. Make a central hole through both circles approximately one-third of the diameter. Place both rings together, one on top of the other, lining up the holes.

2   Thread yarn though a darning needle and wind the yarn through the hole and around the outer edge, ensuring that all the cardboard is covered. Continue until the hole in the centre is completely filled and it is impossible to force the needle through the centre. This will ensure that the pompon is as firm and neat as possible.

3   Ease the two circles of card apart and cut all the strands between the circles. Do not remove the card until a tightly tied double strand of yarn has been secured around the centre of all the strands, leaving a length free to sew the pompon into place. Remove the card and trim any straggly ends of yarn.

moss stitch jacket

Here is a cosy jacket made in a beautiful alpaca and silk yarn to create a luxurious but relaxed jacket for a country weekend.

measurements

To fit bust	82–87	92–97	102–107	cm
	32–34	36–38	40–42	in

actual measurements

Bust	115	130	145	cm
	45¼	51¼	57	in
Length to shoulder	66	67	68	cm
	26	26½	26¾	in
Sleeve length	43	44	45	cm
	17	17¼	17¾	in

materials

24(26:28) 50g balls of Debbie Bliss alpaca silk in Coral
Pair 5mm (US 8) knitting needles
Long 5mm (US 8) circular needle
5 buttons

tension

16 sts and 28 rows to 10cm/4in square over patt using 5mm (US 8) needles.

abbreviations

y2rn = yarn round needle twice to make 2 sts
alt = alternate
beg = beginning
cm = centimetres
cont = continue
foll = following
in = inches
k = knit
p = purl
patt = pattern
rem = remain(ing)
rep = repeat
st st = stocking stitch
st(s) = stitch(es)
tog = together

back   With 5mm (US 8) needles, cast on 94(106:118) sts.

1st row (right side) K2, [p2, k2] to end.

2nd row P2, [k2, p2] to end.

Rep the last 2 rows once more.

Now work in patt as follows:

1st row P2, [k2, p2] to end.

2nd row K2, [p2, k2] to end.

3rd row K2, [p2, k2] to end.

4th row P2, [k2, p2] to end.

These 4 rows form the patt and are repeated throughout.

Cont in patt until back measures 66(67:68)cm/26(26½:26¾)in from beg, ending with a wrong side row.

Shape shoulders

Cast off 16(19:21) sts at beg of next 2 rows and 17(19:22) sts at beg of foll 2 rows.

Cast off rem 28(30:32) sts.

pocket   With 5mm (US 8) needles, cast on 27 sts.

linings   Beg with a k row, work 18cm/7in in st st, ending with a p row and decreasing 3

(make 2)   sts evenly across last row. 24 sts. Leave sts on a holder.

left front   With 5mm (US 8) needles, cast on 43(51:59) sts.

1st row (right side) K2, [p2, k2] to last 5 sts, p2, k3.

2nd row P3, [k2, p2] to end.

Rep the last 2 rows once more.

Work in patt as follows:

1st row P2, [k2, p2] to last 5 sts, k2, p3.

2nd row K3, [p2, k2] to end.

3rd row K2, [p2, k2] to last 5 sts, p2, k3.

4th row P3, [k2, p2] to end.

These 4 rows form the patt and are repeated throughout.

Cont in patt until front measures 20cm/8in from cast-on edge, ending with a wrong side row.

Pocket opening

Next row Patt 12(16:20), cast off next 24 sts in patt, patt to end.

Next row Patt 7(11:15), work in patt across 24 sts of pocket lining, patt to end.

Cont in patt until front measures same as Back to shoulder shaping, ending at side edge.

Shape shoulders

Cast off 16(19:21) sts at beg of next row and 17(19:22) sts at beg of foll alt row.

Leave rem 10(13:16) sts on a holder.

right front

With 5mm (US 8) needles, cast on 43(51:59) sts.

1st row (right side) K3, [p2, k2] to end.

2nd row P2, [k2, p2] to last 5 sts, k2, p3.

Rep the last 2 rows once more.

Work in patt as follows:

1st row P3, [k2, p2] to end.

2nd row K2, [p2, k2] to last 5 sts, p2, k3.

3rd row K3, [p2, k2] to end.

4th row P2, [k2, p2] to last 5 sts, k2, p3.

These 4 rows form the patt and are repeated throughout.

Cont in patt until front measures 20cm/8in from cast-on edge, ending with a wrong side row.

Pocket opening

Next row Patt 7(11:15), cast off next 24 sts in patt, patt to end.

Next row Patt 12(16:20), work in patt across 24 sts of pocket lining, patt to end.

Cont in patt until front measures same as Back to shoulder shaping, ending at side edge.

Shape shoulders

Cast off 16(19:21) sts at beg of next row and 17(19:22) sts at beg of foll alt row.

Leave rem 10(13:16) sts on a holder.

sleeves

With 5mm (US 8) needles, cast on 46(50:54) sts.

Work 4 rows rib as given for Back.

Cont in patt as given for Back and inc one st at each end of the 5th and every foll 8th row until there are 72(76:80) sts.

Cont straight until sleeve measures 43(44:45)cm/17(17¼:17¾)in from cast-on edge, ending with a wrong side row.

Cast off.

collar

Join shoulder seams.

With right side facing and 5mm (US 8) needles, slip 10(13:16) sts from right front onto a needle, cast on 48(50:52) sts for centre back neck, then patt across 10(13:16) sts from left front. 68(76:84) sts.

Work 15cm/6in in patt across all sts, as set by sts from front holders.

Cast off.

button band　On the left front, mark a point 35cm/14in down from cast-off edge of collar. With wrong side of jacket facing and 5mm (US 8) needles, pick up and k75 sts from marker to cast-off edge of collar. Break off yarn and slip these sts onto the 5mm (US 8) circular needle.

With right side of jacket facing and using the same 5mm (US 8) circular needle, pick up and k91(91:95) sts from marker to cast-on edge. 166(166:170) sts.

Work backwards and forwards in rib as follows:

1st row (wrong side) P2, [k2, p2] to end.

2nd row K2, [p2, k2] to end.

Rep the last 2 rows 8 times more.

Cast off in rib.

buttonhole band　On the right front, mark a point 35cm/14in down from cast-off edge of collar. With wrong side of jacket facing and 5mm (US 8) needles, pick up and k75 sts from cast-off edge of collar to marker. Break off yarn and leave sts on needle.

With right side of jacket facing and 5mm (US 8) circular needle, pick up and k91(91:95) sts from cast-on edge to marker. Break off yarn, slip sts from needle onto the circular needle. 166(166:170) sts.

Rejoin yarn to other end of circular needle at the cast-on edge.

Work backwards and forwards in rib as follows:

1st row (right side) K2, [p2, k2] to end.

2nd row P2, [k2, p2] to end.

Rep the last 2 rows 3 times more.

Buttonhole row (right side) Rib 4, [k2tog, y2rn, p2tog tbl, rib 14, p2tog, y2rn, skpo, rib 14] once more, k2tog, y2rn, p2tog tbl, rib to end.

Work a further 9 rows in rib.

Cast off in rib.

to make up　With centre of cast-off edge of sleeve to shoulder, sew on sleeves. Sew cast-on edge of collar to cast-off sts of centre back neck, easing in fullness. Slipstitch pocket linings in place. Join side and sleeve seams. Sew on buttons.

moss stitch wrap

Relax into the perfect snuggly throw that is worked in a soft alpaca blend to create

real cosiness and warmth. Every home needs one.

size
45 x 170cm/17¾ x 67in.

materials
Twelve 50g balls of Debbie Bliss alpaca silk
in Plum
Pair 5½mm (US 9) knitting needles

tension
15 sts and 31 rows to 10cm/4in square over
moss st using 5½mm (US 9) needles.

abbreviations
cm = centimetres
in = inches
k = knit
p = purl
rep = repeat
st(s) = stitch(es)

to make   With 5½mm (US 9) needles, cast on 67 sts.
Moss st row K1, [p1, k1] to end.
Rep this row until throw measures 170cm/67in.
Cast off in moss st.

pan handler

Here is a wonderfully easy knit to make. Worked in moss stitch and lined with a
contrast fabric, it is a practical item that adds a homely touch to your kitchen.

size
18 x 18cm/7 x 7in

materials
One 50g ball of Debbie Bliss cotton dk in
Taupe
Pair 5mm (US 8) knitting needles
20 x 20cm/7¾ x 7¾in piece of fabric
13cm/5in tape or ribbon

tension
17 sts and 24 rows to 10cm/4in square over
moss st using 5mm (US 8) needles and two
strands of yarn.

abbreviations
cm = centimetres
in = inches
k = knit
p = purl
st(s) = stitch(es)

to make   Wind off 25g of yarn into a separate ball, so making two equal balls of yarn.
With 5mm (US 8) needles and the two balls of yarn used together, cast
on 27 sts.
Moss st row K1, [p1, k1] to end.
Rep this row 41 times more.
Cast off in moss st.

lining   Fold tape/ribbon in half to form a loop and stitch to the wrong side of one
corner of the knitted piece. Press 1.5cm/⅝in onto the wrong side of the fabric
on all edges, mitring the corners. Slipstitch the fabric in place to the wrong side
of the knitted piece, 5mm/¼in in from the edges, covering the ends of the
tape/ribbon.

ribbed scarf

This quick and easy scarf is knitted in a space-dyed yarn that creates rustic tonal

effects without having to use more than one yarn.

size
Approximately 12 x 150cm/4¾ x 59in, without
stretching.

materials
Two 100g hanks of Debbie Bliss maya or four
50g balls of Debbie Bliss SoHo shade 06
Pair 5½mm (US 9) knitting needles

tension
25 sts and 24 rows to 10cm/4in square over
unstretched patt using 5½mm (US 9) needles.

abbreviations
cm = centimetres
in = inches
k = knit
p = purl
patt = pattern
st(s) = stitch(es)

to make   With 5½mm (US 9) needles, cast on 31 sts.
1st row [K2, p2] to last 3 sts, k2, p1.
This row forms the patt and is repeated throughout.
Work in patt until scarf measures approximately 150cm/59in from cast-on edge,
or until you have used almost two whole hanks or four balls.
Cast off in patt.

washcloth

This has to be the simplest of items to make. Worked throughout in knit stitches, it is a perfect first project for a beginner.

size
18 x 15cm/7 x 6in.

materials
One 50g ball of Debbie Bliss cotton dk in Cream
Pair 6½mm (US 10½) knitting needles

tension
14 sts and 25 rows to 10cm/4in square over garter st using 6½mm (US 10½) needles and two strands of yarn used together.

abbreviations
cm = centimetres
in = inches
k = knit
st(s) = stitch(es)

to make   Wind off 25g of yarn into a separate ball, so making two equal balls of yarn.
With 6½mm (US 10½) needles and the two balls of yarn used together, cast on 25 sts.
Work 36 rows in garter st (k every row).
Cast off.
Make a small hanging loop on one corner of the washcloth.

woven cushion

This simple cushion is decorated by weaving in a contrast yarn. The yarn used here is space-dyed, which creates a subtle shaded effect.

size
Approximately 40cm/16in square.

materials
Five 50g balls of Debbie Bliss cashmerino aran in Stone (A)
One 100g hank of Debbie Bliss maya (B) in shade 06 or two 50g balls of Debbie Bliss SoHo (B)
Pair 5mm (US 8) knitting needles
40cm/16in square cushion pad

tension
18 sts and 24 rows to 10cm/4in square over st st using 5mm (US 8) needles.

abbreviations
cm = centimetres
in = inches
k = knit
p = purl
patt = pattern
rep = repeat
st st = stocking stitch
st(s) = stitch(es)

to make   With 5mm (US 8) needles and A, cast on 73 sts.

K 3 rows.

Beg with a k row, work 25cm/9¾in in st st, ending with a k row.

Ridge row (wrong side) Knit.

Now work in patt as follows:

1st row (right side) [K3, p1, k2] to last st, k1.

2nd row Purl.

3rd row K1, [p1, k1] to end.

4th row Purl.

5th and 6th rows As 3rd and 4th rows.

7th to 10th rows Rep 1st and 2nd rows twice more.

Repeat these 10 rows 9 times more, then work 1st to 5th rows once more.

Ridge row (wrong side) Knit.

Beg with a k row, work in st st for a further 24cm/9½in, ending with a k row.

K 2 rows.

Cast off knitwise.

to make   Fold the cushion cover in three along the two ridge rows with the cast-on and
up   cast-off edges overlapping to form the opening for the cushion back. Join the
side seams. Insert the cushion pad first, then thread double lengths of contrast
yarn B vertically and horizontally through the cover using the grid pattern as a
guide. By working with the pad inside the cover, you will not pull the threaded
yarn too tight or leave it too loose.

seaside

diagonal front jacket

This casual jacket's unusual structure is created by simply increasing and decreasing to form diagonal ribbed fronts.

measurements

To fit bust	81–92	97–107	cm
	32–36	38–42	in

actual measurements

Bust	100	116	cm
	39½	45½	in
Length	54	63	cm
	21¼	24¾	in
Sleeve seam (with cuff turned back)			
	44	48	cm
	17¼	19	in

materials

16(18) 50g balls of Debbie Bliss cotton dk in Pale Blue
Pair 4mm (US 6) knitting needles
Long 4mm (US 6) circular needle

tension

19 sts and 28 rows to 10cm/4in square over patt using 4mm (US 6) needles.

abbreviations

cm = centimetres
cont = continue
dec = decreas(e)ing
foll = following
in = inches
inc = increas(e)ing
k = knit
kfb = k into front and back of st
m1 = make one by picking up loop lying between st just worked and next st and working into the back of it
p = purl
patt = pattern
rem = remain(ing)
sl = slip
st(s) = stitch(es)
tbl = through back of loop
tog = together

basic	**1st row** (right side) K3, [p1, k3] to end.
stitch	**2nd row** Purl.
pattern	These 2 rows form the basic stitch pattern.

back and (Worked in one piece to armholes)

fronts With 4mm (US 6) circular needle, cast on 215(247) sts.

1st row (right side) K59(67), kfb, [k3, p1] 23(27) times, k2, kfb, k2tog tbl, turn.

Next row Sl 1, p97(113), p2tog, turn.

Next row Sl 1, p1, m1, [k3, p1] 23(27) times, k3, m1, p1, k1, k2tog tbl, turn.

Next row Sl 1, p101(117), p2tog, turn.

Next row Sl 1, k1, p1, k1, m1, [k3, p1] 23(27) times, k3, m1, k1, p1, k2, k2tog tbl, turn.

Next row Sl 1, p105(121), p2tog, turn.

Next row Sl 1, k2, p1, k2, m1, [k3, p1] 23(27) times, k3, m1, k2, p1, k3, k2tog tbl, turn.

Next row Sl 1, p109(125), p2tog, turn.

Next row Sl 1, k3, p1, k3, m1, [k3, p1] 23(27) times, k3, m1, k3, p1, k3, p1, k2tog tbl, turn.

Next row Sl 1, p113(129), p2tog, turn.

Next row Sl 1, p1, [k3, p1] twice, m1, [k3, p1] 23(27) times, k3, m1, [p1, k3] twice, p1, k1, k2tog tbl, turn.

Next row Sl 1, p117(133), p2tog, turn.

Next row Sl 1, k1, p1, [k3, p1] twice, k1, m1, [k3, p1] 23(27) times, k3, m1, k1, [p1, k3] twice, p1, k2, k2tog tbl, turn.

Next row Sl 1, p121(137), p2tog, turn.

These turning rows set the way in which cast-on sts are taken into work at each side for the Fronts. Cont to inc one st at each side of centre 95(111) sts on every right side row and work 2 more sts tog at end of every row, slipping the previous row's worked tog st at beg of every row. Cont in this way until all cast-on sts have been worked and taken into the basic stitch patt, so ending with a wrong side row.

Cont to inc one st at each side of centre 95(111) sts on next and every foll right side row taking inc sts into patt and working p1 at each end of every right side row, until there are 223(255) sts, ending with a wrong side p row.

Next row (right side) P2tog, patt 62(70), m1, patt 95(111), m1, patt 62(70), p2tog.

Next row Purl.

Keeping patt correct, rep the last 2 rows 11(19) times more, ending with a p row.

right front

Divide for Back and Fronts

Next row (right side) With 4mm (US 6) needles, p2tog, patt 62(70), turn and cont on these sts only, leave rem sts on the circular needle.

Next row (wrong side) P63(71).

Next row P2tog, patt 61(69).

Next row P62(70).

Next row P2tog, patt 60(68).

Cont in this way to dec one st at beg of every right side row until 32(36) sts rem, ending with a p row.

Do not cut yarn, leave sts on a holder.

back

With right side facing, 4mm (US 6) needles and a new ball of yarn, work across rem sts on circular needle as follows: k3, p2tog, patt 85(101), p2tog, k3, turn and cont on these 93(109) sts only, leave rem sts on the circular needle.

Next row (wrong side) P93(109).

Next row K3, p2tog, patt 83(99), p2tog, k3.

Next row P91(107).

Next row K3, p2tog, patt 81(97), p2tog, k3.

Cont in this way to dec one st at each end of every right side row until 31(39) sts rem, ending with a p row.

Cut yarn and leave sts on a holder.

left front

With right side facing and 4mm (US 6) needles, rejoin yarn to rem sts on circular needle, patt to last 2 sts, p2tog.

Next row (wrong side) Purl.

Next row Patt to last 2 sts, p2tog.

Cont in this way to dec one st at end of every foll right side row until 32(36) sts rem, ending with a p row.

Leave sts on a holder.

sleeves

Cuff

With 4mm (US 6) needles, cast on 43(47) sts.

1st row (right side) K1, [p1, k3] to last 2 sts, p1, k1.

2nd row Purl.

These 2 rows set the patt.

Work in patt until sleeve measures 8cm/3¼in, ending with a right side row.

Ridge row (wrong side) Knit.

Next row (right side) Knit.

Now reverse the patt for the main sleeve as follows:

Next row (right side) K1, [p1, k3] to last 2 sts, p1, k1.

Next row Purl.

Cont in patt as set for a further 8cm/3¼in, ending with a p row.

Next row (right side) K1, m1, patt to last st, m1, k1.

Cont in patt and inc one st in the same way, at each end of every foll 4th row until there are 75(71) sts, then at each end of every foll 6th row until there are 83(87) sts.

Cont straight until sleeve measures 44(48)cm/17¼(19)in from ridge row, ending with a p row.

Shape raglans

Next row (right side) K1, p2tog, patt to last 3 sts, p2tog, k1.

Next row Purl.

Rep these 2 rows until 19(15) sts rem, ending with a p row.

Leave sts on a holder.

collar With right side facing and 4mm (US 6) circular needle, work across sts on holders as follows: work p2tog, patt 29(33) across right front, k last st tog with first st of right sleeve, [p1, k3] 4(3) times, p1, k last st tog with first st of back, k2, [p1, k3] 6(8) times, p1, k2, k last st tog with first st of left sleeve, [p1, k3] 4(3) times, p1, k last st tog with first st of left front, k2, patt to last 2 sts, p2tog. 125(137) sts.

Next row (wrong side) Purl.

Next row (right side) P2tog, patt to last 2 sts, p2tog.

Rep these 2 rows until collar measures 8cm/3¼in, ending with a right side row. Cast off knitwise.

to make up Join raglan seams, matching row for row. Join sleeve seams.

child's denim sweater

This very easy child's sweater in my denim yarn knits up quickly and simply and so is ideal for the novice knitter.

measurements

To fit ages	2	3	4	years
actual measurements				
Chest	71	80	88	cm
	28	31½	34¾	in
Length	35	38	42	cm
	13¾	15	16½	in
Sleeve seam	22	25	28	cm
	8¾	9¾	11	in

materials

6(7:8) 50g balls of Debbie Bliss cotton denim aran in Medium Blue
Pair each 4mm (US 6) and 4½mm (US 7) knitting needles

tension

18 sts and 24 rows to 10cm/4in square over st st using 4½mm (US 7) needles.

abbreviations

beg = beginning
cm = centimetres
cont = continue
dec = decreas(e)ing
foll = following
in = inches
inc = increas(e)ing
k = knit
p = purl
rem = remain(ing)
st st = stocking stitch
st(s) = stitch(es)

back and front   With 4½mm (US 7) needles, cast on 66(74:82) sts.

Beg with a k row, work 6 rows in st st.

Next row K2, [p2, k2] to end.

Next row P2, [k2, p2] to end.

Rep the last 2 rows once more.

Beg with a k row, work in st st until back/front measures 31(34:38)cm/
12¼(13¼:15)in from cast-on edge, ending with a wrong side row.

Shape neck

Next row K24(27:30) sts, turn and work on these sts for first side of neck,
leave rem sts on a spare needle.

Dec one st at neck edge of next 6 rows.

Work 3 rows.

Cast off.

With right side facing, slip centre 18(20:22) sts onto a holder, rejoin yarn to rem sts, k to end.

Dec one st at neck edge of next 6 rows.

Work 3 rows.

Cast off.

sleeves   With 4mm (US 6) needles, cast on 34(38:42) sts.

Beg with a k row, work 6 rows st st.

Next row K2, [p2, k2] to end.

Next row P2, [k2, p2] to end.

Rep the last 2 rows once more.

Change to 4½mm (US 7) needles.

Beg with a k row, work in st st and inc one st at each end of the 3rd and every foll 4th row until there are 50(58:66) sts.

Cont straight until sleeve measures 20(23:26)cm/7¾ (9:10¼)in from cast-on edge, ending with a p row.

Next row K2, [p2, k2] to end.

Next row P2, [k2, p2] to end.

Rep the last 2 rows once more.

Cast off.

neckband   Join right shoulder seam.

With right side facing and 4½mm (US 7) needles, pick up and k10 sts down left front neck, k across 18(20:22) sts from front neck holder, pick up and k9 sts up right front neck and 9 sts down right back neck, k across 18(20:22) sts from back neck holder, then pick up and k10 sts up left back neck. 74(78:82) sts.

Next row K2, [p2, k2] to end.

Next row P2, [k2, p2] to end.

Rep the last 2 rows once more.

Beg with a p row, work 5 rows st st.

Cast off.

to make   Join left shoulder and neckband seam. With centre of cast-off edge of sleeve to
up   shoulder, sew on sleeves. Join side and sleeve seams.

cushion with denim ties

A simple stocking stitch cushion in a crisp white cotton is embellished with fabric

bows made from soft, jeans-look fabric.

size
Approximately 40cm/16in square.

materials
Six 50g balls of Debbie Bliss cotton dk
in White
Pair 4mm (US 6) knitting needles
40cm/16in square cushion pad
Strips of washed denim fabric

tension
20 sts and 28 rows to 10cm/4in square over
st st using 4mm (US 6) needles.

abbreviations
beg = beginning
cm = centimetres
cont = continue
in = inches
k = knit
st st = stocking stitch
st(s) = stitch(es)

to make
With 4mm (US 6) needles, cast on 83 sts.
K 3 rows.
Beg with a k row, work 25cm/9¾in in st st, ending with a k row.
Ridge row (wrong side) Knit.
Beg with a k row, cont in st st and work a further 40cm/16in, ending with a
k row.
Ridge row (wrong side) Knit.
Beg with a k row, cont in st st and work a further 24cm/9½in, ending with a
k row.
K 2 rows.
Cast off knitwise.

to make up
Fold the cushion cover in three along the ridge rows, with the cast-on and cast-off edges overlapping to form the opening for the cushion back. Join the side seams and insert the cushion pad. Thread 13cm/5in lengths of denim through the cushion front and tie.

floor cushions

These floor cushions are perfect for creating a relaxed, comfortable atmosphere.

They are inspired by stitch patterning on classic fishermen's sweaters.

garter stitch detail floor cushion

size
Approximately 65cm/25½in square.

materials
Seven 50g balls of Debbie Bliss cotton dk
in Navy
Pair 4mm (US 6) knitting needles
66 x 70cm/26 x 27½in fabric for cushion back
50cm/20in zip fastener
66–70cm/26–28in square cushion pad

tension
18 sts and 28 rows to 10cm/4in square over
patt using 4mm (US 6) needles.

abbreviations
cm = centimetres
in = inches
k = knit
p = purl
patt = pattern
rep = repeat
st(s) = stitch(es)

cushion front

With 4mm (US 6) needles, cast on 117 sts.

1st row (right side) K5, [p3, k5] to end.

2nd row Purl.

Rep these 2 rows until cushion front measures 65cm/25½in from cast-on edge, ending with a right side row.

Cast off.

cushion back

Cut two 66 x 35cm/26 x 13¾in pieces of fabric. With right sides together, pin and tack-stitch the two pieces together along one long edge, taking a 2cm/¾in seam. Remove pins and machine stitch for 8cm/3¼in at each end of the seam, leaving the centre 50cm/20in unstitched for zip placement. Press seam open. Lay zip face down onto the wrong side of the pressed seam and tack in place. From the right side, topstitch the zip in place. Remove all tacking threads.

to make up

Open the zip slightly and, with right sides together, lay the knitted cushion front onto the cushion back and stitch around the edge. Open the zip, turn through and insert cushion pad, close zip.

Guernsey floor cushion

size
Approximately 65cm/25½in square.

materials
Eight 50g balls of Debbie Bliss cotton dk in
Pale Blue
Pair 4mm (US 6) knitting needles
66 x 70cm/26 x 27½in fabric for cushion back
50cm/20in zip fastener
66–70cm/26–28in square cushion pad

tension
20 sts and 28 rows to 10cm/4in square over
st st using 4mm (US 6) needles.

abbreviations
beg = beginning
C4F = slip next 2 sts onto a cable needle and
hold at front of work, k2, then k2 from cable
needle
cm = centimetres
dec = decreas(e)ing
in = inches
k = knit
p = purl
patt = pattern
st st = stocking stitch
st(s) = stitch(es)

pattern
panel A
(worked
over 15 sts)

1st row (right side) K1, p13, k1.

2nd row P1, k13, p1.

3rd row As 1st row.

4th row P15.

5th row K15.

6th row P7, k1, p7.

7th row K6, p1, k1, p1, k6.

8th row P5, k1, p3, k1, p5.

9th row K4, p1, [k2, p1] twice, k4.

10th row P3, k1, p2, k1, p1, k1, p2, k1, p3.

11th row [K2, p1] twice, k3, [p1, k2] twice.

12th row P4, k1, [p2, k1] twice, p4.

13th row K3, p1, k2, p1, k1, p1, k2, p1, k3.

14th row As 8th row.

15th row As 9th row.

16th row P6, k1, p1, k1, p6.

17th row K5, p1, k3, p1, k5.

18th row As 6th row.

19th row K6, p3, k6.

20th row As 6th row.

21st row As 5th row.

22nd row As 4th row.

These 22 rows form Patt Panel A.

pattern
panel B
(worked
over 13 sts)

1st row (right side) K1, p11, k1.

2nd row P1, k11, p1.

3rd row As 1st row.

4th row P13.

5th row K13.

6th row P6, k1, p6.

7th row K5, p1, k1, p1, k5.

8th row P4, k1, [p1, k1] twice, p4.

9th row K3, p1, [k1, p1] 3 times, k3.

10th row P2, k1, [p1, k1] 4 times, p2.

11th row K1, [p1, k1] 6 times.

12th row As 10th row.

13th row As 9th row.

14th row As 8th row.

15th row As 7th row.

16th row As 6th row.

17th row As 5th row.

18th row As 4th row.

These 18 rows form Patt Panel B.

pattern **1st row** (right side) K1, p7, k1.

panel C **2nd row** P1, k7, p1.

(worked **3rd row** As 1st row.

over 9 sts) **4th row** P5, k2, p2.

5th row K3, p2, k4.

6th row P3, k2, p4.

7th row K5, p2, k2.

8th row P1, k2, p6.

9th row K6, p2, k1.

10th row P2, k2, p5.

11th row K4, p2, k3.

12th row P4, k2, p3.

13th row K2, p2, k5.

14th row P6, k2, p1.

15th row K1, p2, k6.

The 4th to 15th rows form Patt Panel C.

pattern **1st row** K4.

panel D **2nd row** P4.

(worked **3rd row** C4F.

over 4 sts) **4th row** P4.

5th and 6th rows As 1st and 2nd rows.

These 6 rows form Patt Panel D.

cushion With 4mm (US 6) needles, cast on 118 sts.

front Beg with a k row, work 17cm/6¾in in st st, ending with a p row and inc 9 sts
evenly across last row. 127 sts.

Now work in patt as follows:

1st row (right side) P1, k1, p1, work across 1st row Patt Panel A, p1, k1, p1,
work across 1st row Patt Panel B, p1, k1, p1, work across 1st row Patt Panel
C, p1, k1, p1, work across 1st row Patt Panel D, p1, k1, p1, work across 1st
row Patt Panel A, p1, k1, p1, work across 1 st row Patt Panel D, p1, k1, p1,
work across 1st row Patt Panel C, p1, k1, p1, work across 1st row Patt Panel
B, p1, k1, p1, work across 1st row Patt Panel A, p1, k1, p1.

This row sets the position of the patt panels with 3 moss sts between each panel.

Cont in patt as set, working correct patt panel rows, until 6 repeats of Patt Panel A have been worked, so ending with a wrong side row.

Next row (right side) P and dec 9 sts evenly across row.

Next row Knit.

Next 2 rows Purl.

Next 2 rows Knit.

Next row Purl.

Next 2 rows Knit.

Next row Purl.

Next row Knit.

Next row Purl.

Cast off.

cushion back   Cut two 66 x 35cm/26 x 13¾in pieces of fabric. With right sides together, pin and tack-stitch the two pieces together along one long edge, taking a 2cm/¾in seam. Remove pins and machine stitch for 8cm/3¼in at each end of the seam, leaving the centre 50cm/20in unstitched for zip placement. Press seam open. Lay zip face down onto the wrong side of the pressed seam and tack in place. From the right side, topstitch the zip in place. Remove all tacking threads.

to make up   Open the zip slightly and, with right sides together, lay the knitted cushion front onto the cushion back and stitch around the edge. Open the zip, turn through and insert cushion pad, close zip.

peg bag

A lining made from a bright and cheerful spotty fabric contrasts with the texture of

this practical moss stitch peg bag.

size
Approximately 26 x 30cm/10 x 12in.

materials
Three 50g balls of Debbie Bliss cotton dk
in White
Pair 4mm (US 6) knitting needles
34 x 55cm/13 x 21¾in piece of fabric for lining
Sewing thread
30cm/12in plain wooden coathanger

tension
20 sts and 33 rows to 10cm/4in square over
moss st using 4mm (US 6) needles.

abbreviations
cm = centimetres
in = inches
k = knit
p = purl
st(s) = stitch(es)

to make   With 4mm (US 6) needles, cast on 61 sts.

Moss st row K1, [p1, k1] to end.

This row forms moss st and is repeated throughout.

Work in moss st for 46cm/18in, ending with a right side row.

Next row Moss st 16, cast off next 29 sts knitwise, moss st to end.

Next row Work in moss st and cast on 29 sts over cast-off sts of previous row.

Work a further 6cm/2½in in moss st, ending with a right side row.

Cast off knitwise.

Fold in half and join side seams.

lining   Fold fabric in half widthways, then, taking a 1.5cm/⅝in allowance, join the seam for 9.5cm/3¾in at each end, leaving a central 15cm/6in gap. Press seam open. Refold so that seam is placed 6cm/2¼in below top fold. Press along folds. Taking 1.5cm/⅝in seams, join one side seam for the full length and then join the other side seam leaving a gap in the seam just large enough to insert the hanger. Make a small hole in the centre of the top fold for the hanger hook and insert the hanger. Close gap in side seam. Insert lining with hanger into the knitted section and join the top seam on either side of the hook. Slipstitch lining to knitting around front opening.

moss stitch rug

A cotton denim-style yarn worked double creates a soft but sturdy fabric, which is

perfect for a rug or beach blanket.

size
72.5 x 92cm/28½ x 36in.

materials
Seventeen 50g balls of Debbie Bliss cotton
denim aran in Medium Blue
Pair 7mm (US 10½) knitting needles

tension
12 sts and 21 rows to 10cm/4in square over
moss st using 7mm (US 10½) needles and two
strands of yarn.

abbreviations
cm = centimetres
in = inches
k = knit
p = purl
st(s) = stitch(es)

to make   With 7mm (US 10½) needles and two balls of yarn used together, cast on 87 sts.
Moss st row K1, [p1, k1] to end.
This row forms moss st and is repeated throughout.
Work in moss st until rug measures 92cm/36in.
Cast off in moss st.
Darn in all yarn ends.

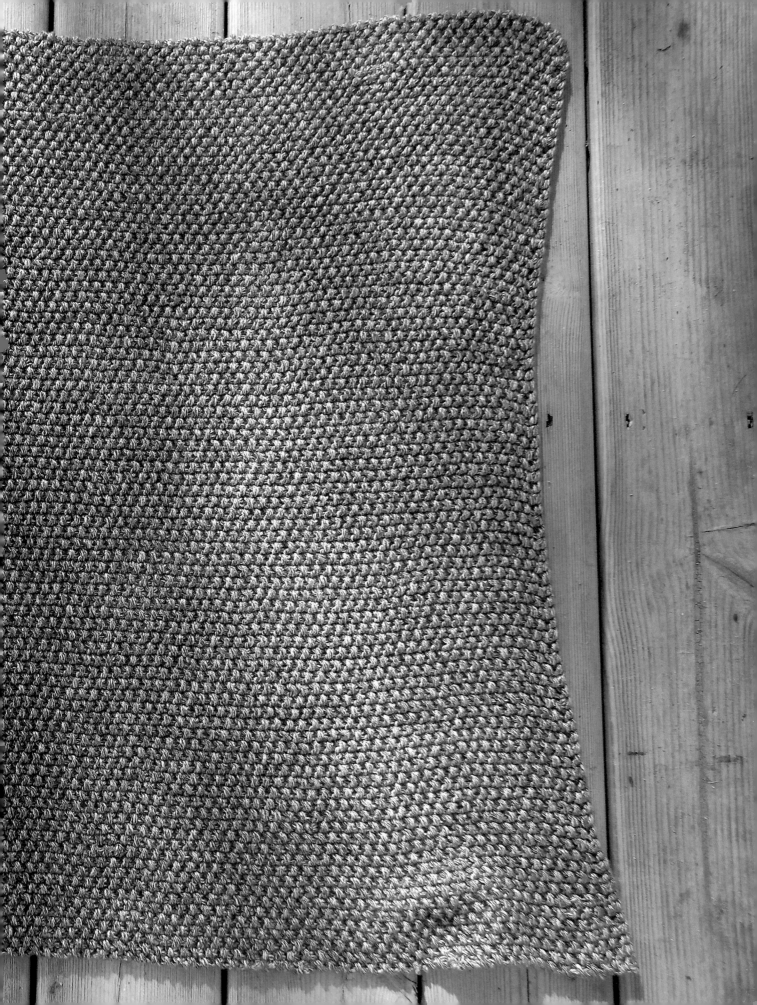

seaside throw

Here is a throw that uses traditional Guernsey patterns with lace and bobbles. The cotton yarn gives clarity to the stitch detail.

size

Approximately 90 x 130cm/35½in x 51¼in.

materials

Twenty-one 50g balls of Debbie Bliss cotton dk in Pale Blue
Pair each 3¾mm (US 5) and 4mm (US 6) knitting needles

tension

20 sts and 28 rows to 10cm/4in square over st st using 4mm (US 6) needles.

abbreviations

beg = beginning
C4F = slip next 2 sts onto cable needle and hold at front of work, k2, then k2 from cable needle
cm = centimetres
in = inches
k = knit
mb = knit into front and back of next stitch twice, then pass 3rd, 2nd and 1st sts over 4th st, so making bobble
p = purl
patt = pattern
pfb = purl into front and back of next st
rep = repeat
skpo = slip 1, knit 1, pass slipped stitch over
st st = stocking stitch
st(s) = stitch(es)
tog = together
yf = yarn to front of work

pattern panel A (worked over 4 sts)

1st row (right side) K4.

2nd row P4.

3rd and 4th rows As 1st and 2nd rows.

5th row C4F.

6th row P4.

These 6 rows form Patt Panel A.

pattern panel B (worked over 11 sts)

1st row (right side) K11.

2nd row P11.

3rd row K5, p1, k5.

4th row P4, k1, p1, k1, p4.

5th row K3, [p1, k1] twice, p1, k3.

6th row P2, [k1, p1] 3 times, k1, p2.

7th row K1, [p1, k1] 4 times, p1, k1.

8th row As 6th row.

9th row As 5th row.

10th row As 4th row.

11th row As 3rd row.

12th row As 2nd row

13th to 16th rows K11.

These 16 rows form Patt Panel B.

pattern panel C (worked over 11 sts)

1st row (right side) K5, yf, skpo, k4.

2nd and every wrong side row P11.

3rd row K3, k2tog, yf, k1, yf, skpo, k3.

5th row K2, k2tog, yf, k3, yf, skpo, k2.

7th row K1, k2tog, yf, k2, mb, k2, yf, skpo, k1.

8th row P11.

These 8 rows form Patt Panel C.

to make

With 3¾mm (US 5) needles, cast on 168 sts.

1st row (right side) [K1, p1] to end.

2nd row [P1, k1] to end.

3rd to 7th rows Rep 1st and 2nd rows twice more, then 1st row again.

Inc row (wrong side) Moss st 5, [pfb, pfb, moss st 37] 4 times, pfb, pfb, moss st 5. 178 sts.

Change to 4mm (US 6) needles.

Now work in pattern as follows:

1st row (right side) Moss st 5, [work 1st row Patt Panel A, moss st 5, work 1st row Patt Panel B, moss st 5, work 1st row Patt Panel C, moss st 5] 4 times, work 1st row Patt Panel A, moss st 5.

2nd row Moss st 5, [work 2nd row Patt Panel A, moss st 5, work 2nd row Patt Panel C, moss st 5, work 2nd row Patt Panel B, moss st 5] 4 times, work 2nd row Patt Panel A, moss st 5.

These 2 rows set the position of the pattern panels with moss st between.

Cont in patt until work measures approximately 128cm/50½in from beg, ending with a 12th row of Patt Panel B.

Change to 3¾mm (US 5) needles.

Dec row (right side) Moss st 5, [work 2tog, work 2tog, moss st 37] 4 times, k2tog, p2tog, moss st 5. 168 sts.

Work 7 rows in moss st.

Cast off.

tote bag

What a great bag for the beach or picnics. This one is large enough to contain your favourite book, specs and lunch. An additional pocket on the outside can house your mobile phone, too.

size

Approximately 37 x 22cm/14½ x 8¾in.

materials

Six 50g balls of Debbie Bliss cotton dk in White
Pair 4mm (US 6) knitting needles
One 4mm (US 6) circular needle
50cm/½yd of 112cm/44in wide fabric for lining

tension

20 sts and 28 rows to 10cm/4in square over st st using 4mm (US 6) needles.

abbreviations

cm = centimetres
cont = continue
in = inches
inc = increas(e)ing
k = knit
kfb = k into front and back of st
p = purl
rep = repeat
sl = slip
st st = stocking stitch
st(s) = stitch(es)
tog = together
yf = yarn to front of work

pocket lining	With 4mm (US 6) needles, cast on 21 sts. Beg with a k row, work 26 rows in st st. Leave sts on a holder.
base	With 4mm (US 6) circular needle, cast on 5 sts. **1st row** (right side) [Kfb] 4 times, k1. 9 sts. **2nd and all wrong side rows** Purl. **3rd row** [Kfb] 8 times, k1. 17 sts. **5th row** [K1, kfb] 8 times, k1. 25 sts. **7th row** [K2, kfb] 8 times, k1. 33 sts. **9th row** [K3, kfb] 8 times, k1. 41 sts. Cont to work in st st and inc 8 sts across every right side row as set, working one st more before each inc as set until there are 137 sts, ending with a right side row.
main bag	**Ridge row** (wrong side) Knit. **Next row** Knit. **Next 2 rows** K1, [p1, k1] to end. **Next row** *K1, [p1, k1] 3 times, p3; rep from * to last 7 sts, [k1, p1] 3 times, k1. **Next row** K1, *[p1, k1] twice, p1, k5; rep from * to last 6 sts, [p1, k1] 3 times. **Next row** P2, *k1, p1, k1, p7; rep from * to last 5 sts, k1, p1, k1, p2. **Next row** K3, *p1, k9; rep from * to last 4 sts, p1, k3. Beg with a p row, cont straight in st st until work measures 27cm/10¾in from ridge row, ending with a p row. **Place pocket** **Next row** K58, sl next 21 sts onto a holder, k across 21 sts from pocket lining, k to end. Cont in st st until work measures 35cm/13¾in from ridge row, ending with a p row. **Next row** (right side) K3, *p1, k9; rep from * to last 4 sts, p1, k3. **Next row** P2, *k1, p1, k1, p7; rep from * to last 5 sts, k1, p1, k1, p2. **Next row** K1, *[p1, k1] twice, p1, k5; rep from * to last 6 sts, [p1, k1] 3 times.

Next row *K1, [p1, k1] 3 times, p3; rep from * to last 7 sts, [k1, p1] 3 times, k1.
Next 2 rows K1, [p1, k1] to end.
K 1 row.
P 1 row.
Eyelet row (right side) K4, yf, k2tog, k to last 6 sts, k2tog, yf, k4.
P 1 row.
K 1 row.
Ridge row (wrong side) Knit.
Beg with a p row, work 4 rows.
Cast off.

pocket top

With right side facing and 4mm (US 6) needles, work across 21 sts from pocket holder as follows:
Moss st row K1, [p1, k1] to end.
Rep this row 4 times more.
Cast off knitwise.

to make up

Stitch pocket lining and edges of pocket top in place. Join seam in base and cont to cast-off edge. Fold top over onto wrong side along ridge row and slipstitch the hem in place. Make a plait/braid approximately 130cm/51in long from 6 strands of yarn, tie each end of the plait and thread through the top hem from one eyelet to the other. Tie together the ends of the plait.

lining

Cut a 22cm/8¾in circle from strong cardboard (use a plate or bowl to draw around) for the base. Using the card base as a template, cut a circle from fabric allowing an extra 1.5cm/⅝in all around. Place cardboard base into the knitted bag. Cut a 72 x 39cm/28¼ x 15¼in piece of fabric, fold in half and stitch into a tube along the shorter sides, taking a 1.5cm/⅝in seam. Stitch circular fabric base into one end of the tube. Press a 1.5cm/⅝in hem onto the wrong side of the open end, insert into the knitted bag, aligning the seams, and slipstitch around the top.

yarn distributors

For Debbie Bliss yarn stockist information only, please contact:

UK
Designer Yarns Ltd
Units 8-10 Newbridge Industrial
Estate
Pitt Street
Keighley
W. Yorkshire
BD21 4PQ
UK

Tel: +44 (0)1535 664222
Fax: +44 (0)1535 664333
www.designeryarns.uk.com
e-mail: jane@designeryarns.uk.com

USA
Knitting Fever Inc.
P.O. Box 336
315 Bayview Avenue
Amityville, NY 11701
USA

Tel: 001 516 546 3600
www.knittingfever.com
e-mail:
knittingfever@knittingfever.com

CANADA
Diamond Yarns Ltd
155 Martin Ross Avenue Unit 3
Toronto
Ontario M3J 2L9.
Canada

Tel: 001 416 736 6111
www.diamondyarn.com

MEXICO
Red Color S.A. DE CV.
San Antonio 105
Col. Santa Maria
Monterrey
N.L. 64650
Mexico

Tel: +52 818 173 3700
e-mail: Abremer@starsoft.co.mx

JAPAN
Eisaku Noro & Co Ltd
55 Shimoda Ohibino Azaichou
Ichinomita Aichi
4910105
Japan

Tel: +81 52 203 5100
www.eisakunoro.com

GERMANY/AUSTRIA/
SWITZERLAND
Designer Yarns
Handelsagentur Klaus Koch
Mauritius Str, 130
50226 Frechen
Germany

Tel: +49 (0) 2234 205453
Fax: +49 2234 205456
www.designeryarns.de

FRANCE
Elle Tricote
8 Rue du Coq, La Petit France
67000 Strasbourg
France

Tel: +33 (0)388 230313
www.elletricote.com.fr

SPAIN
Oyambre
Pau Claris 145
08009 Barcelona
Spain

Tel: +34 934 872672
e-mail:
oyambre@oyambreonline.com

BELGIUM/HOLLAND
Pavan
Meerlaanstraat 73
Oostrezele 9860
Belgium

Tel: +32 9221 8594
Fax +32 9221 5662
e-mail: pavan@pandora.be

SWEDEN
Hamilton Design
Långgatan 20
SE-64730 Mariefred
Sweden

Tel: +46 (0)159 12006
www.hamiltondesign.biz

AUSTRALIA
Jo Sharp Pty Ltd
PO Box 1018
Fremantle
WA 6959
Australia

Tel: +61 (0)8 9430 9699
e-mail: yarn@josharp.com.au

For information about Debbie Bliss products and Debbie Bliss *the club,* visit www.debbieblissonline.com

acknowledgements

This book would not have been possible without the invaluable contribution of the following people:

Rosy Tucker, for both her invaluable creative and practical collaboration and her support on this book, including the pattern checking.

Penny Hill, for pattern compiling and for organising her great team of knitters.

Pia Tryde, the photographer, and Julia Bird, the stylist, who created the beautiful look and feel of the book and who, together with Marco, the assistant, made the shoot such a joy to work on.

Sarah Lavelle and Carey Smith at Ebury, for their support and for making the book happen.

Christine Wood, for her great book design.

The wonderful knitters, without whom none of this would have happened: Cynthia Brent, Pat Church, Jacqui Dunt, Penny Hill, Maisie Lawrence, Frances Wallace.

Emma Callery, a perfect and unflappable editor.

Heather Jeeves, my wonderful agent.

The models, Evie, Jo, Madeleine and Rose.

The knitters, retailers and distributors who support my books and yarns.

Thank you to Cath Kidston for the use of her products in the book and to Melanie and Tom Petherick for the use of their beautiful seaside home.

MIDDLESBROUGH LIBRARIES & INFORMATION